FAMILY TREE

JOAQUÍN ZIHUATANEJO

FAMILY TREE

Joaquín Zihuatanejo

Copyright ©2012 by Joaquín Zihuatanejo

First Edition

First Edition September 2012

All rights reserved. No part of any of the poems in this book may be reproduced in any form without the prior written permission of Joaquín Zihuatanejo.

Book design and production by Book Baby and Bonita Blvd Publications.

Cover art, "Tree of Life" by Doug Seaman. Contact artist, Doug Seaman, at DSeaman_inkart@mac.com

Published and manufactured in The United States by Book Baby and Bonita Blvd Publications.

Order the EBook version of Family Tree, Barrio Songs, and OF FIRE AND RAIN by Joaquín Zihuatanejo at Online bookstores everywhere. Order additional books and CDs by Joaquin at www.artspeakspoet.com

This is the story of a boy, a dull ax, and a tree…

Also by Joaquín Zihuatanejo

Books

Barrio Songs

of fire and rain
a collaboration with natasha carrizosa

CDs

Barrio Songs

Stand Up and Be Heard

Live at Longwood

of fire and rain
a spoken word collaboration with natasha carrizosa

Child of the Hood Days

HOPE 5 MILES

Barbaric Yawps
Best of Joaquin Zihuatanejo for Students

Family Tree

forthcoming

Canciones del Barrio
Poemas en la Lengua de mi Abuelo

Contents

Family Tree	1
Something, Nothing, Everything	3
Ode to Sleepwalkers	4
The Bride Sister from Sixteen Candles	5
Karma	6
Lost and Found	7
I'll Never Forget	9
HOPE 5 MILES	10
Final Exam for My Father	11
Reinventing the Enemy's Language	13
Tag	15
Cumbersome	17
By the Numbers	19
Another Kind of Graveyard	23
Clean	24
House Fires	25
For the Jewel Thieves	26
Just After Night Falls	28
Flawed	30
Negative	32
Incongruent	34
It Happens By Fractions	35
Forgetting Jude	36
It Ends the Way It Begins	38
Mix Tape Biographical Sonnets	40
Haiku Interlude	44
Metaphorically Speaking	55
Perfection from Flaw	56
Scarlet Poem	57
Slow Down 'Manito	58
My Tío Juan and His Way with Words	59
The Corner of Beautiful and Tomorrow	61
Celestial Bodies	66
About the Author	67
Family Photos	69
Acknowledgements	74
Homework Assignments	76

I spent years

in my mother's silence,

my father's absence,

my grandfather's garden,

and my wife's embrace.

This book is for each of you,

and all of you.

Family Tree

They say fruit don't fall far from the tree
And I hope that's not true.
Used to think my mother was a willow and my father was an oak
But the tree I fell from is crooked and broke
Split in two by lightening
That's why there's nothing more frightening
Than the sound of my raised voice in the direction of my youngest daughter
You see, I don't ever want her to look at me
The way I imagine I'd look at my father
Right before I slap him across the face
For leaving me in a place
Where oak trees are as scarce as two parent families
Where the first word a hungry child learns is *please*
Ain't no shade under a family tree
When a father leaves
Just boughs as broke
As the vows he spoke
The night he plucked me into existence
They say a tree can only withstand so much resistance
I wonder if you cut my heart in two
And counted the rings from the center to its edge
Would it equal the number of years it's been since you left
You were the taking tree
Took everything you could from her
Took everything you could from me
Left my mother's arms looking for your limbs
And grasping only air
That's why she didn't mind ensnaring men who only pretended to care
Somewhere between the muck and mire
Of a brown girl's fear and white boy's desire
Is where my roots took hold
I was less than a year old
Nothing more than a sapling
When you left me under the shade of the woman my mother used to be
Don't you see father
This is the story of a boy, a dull ax, and a tree
It's taken me years to cut you out of me
Can you imagine the cacophony?
The sound of the blade striking against you
The sound of a family being cut in two
And now that I'm through
I find I'm just as stumped as you
Wondering what to do with the remnants of you?
Shape one of your limbs into a cane?
No, I could never lean on you
Maybe sculpt you into a blood red violin?

No, I wouldn't know where to begin
To find the music in any of this
So I'll carve a coffin from your carcass
Give your absence some purpose
And I'll fill it with poems
Most of them true
And a few of them lies
I could write about your hands
And her eyes
Some will be hellos
But most will be goodbyes
And I'll load you up
Cart you far away from me
Give you a proper burial at sea
And though my muscles may ache from all that weight
I'll walk you out beyond the break
Let the tide take you away from me

Maybe then we'll both be free
Maybe then the world can see

I am the fruit
You are the tree
I fell from you
You failed me
I am the wave
She is the sea
I break away
She breaks me
I am not you
Though you are me,
I am the fruit
That fell far from the tree.

Something, Nothing, Everything

My mother was something to me,
Not a lot but something.
My father was nothing to me,
Not a little but nothing.
My grandfather was everything to me,
Not nothing or something,
But everything.
This is how it is for some of us
Trapped between nothing and something
Yet desperate for everything.
So my mother's eyes were something to me,
While my father's hands were nothing.
Abuelo's garden was everything—
I didn't want her to kneel beside me in the dirt
Some things shouldn't be a part of everything.
When I rub my fingers through soil
Or smell cilantro
Or taste tomato
I might think of my grandfather's voice
Or his smile
Or the wrinkles on both sides of his eyes
But I would never think of my father
When you're a child
Nothing could come between you and everything.

Ode to Sleepwalkers

for Dakota

In *Harry Potter and the Half Blood Prince*,
We see that *Luna Lovegood* wears her shoes to bed.

Why?

Because she's a sleepwalker.

So was Lady Macbeth,
And so is my youngest daughter

And blessed are these vampirical creatures
Who rise with the moon to teach us all they know about darkness and faith
Their hands buried in pockets
Or at their side,
Not outstretched
Feeling for the obnoxious wall or inconsiderate doorknob
No, not that,
They believe in the path that they walk so whole-heartedly
That they don't have to see it
They can feel it
Under their feet
In their hearts
Coursing through their veins
It's knowing you've got nothing to lose
And everything to gain
If you could just
Trust yourself
If you could believe in the possibility of making your way through the darkness

So live as the sleepwalkers do
Take a deep breath
Take that first step
And know
With every fiber of your being
That there is so much more to believing
Than simply seeing

The Bride Sister from Sixteen Candles

for Aida

On the night we wed
You said
Pour me...one more
One more time than you should have
You turned into the bride sister
From Sixteen Candles
All slur and stumble
You refused to take your wedding dress off
Because as you said
Between sobs
I look so...damn...pretty
Why are you crying I asked
Don't blame me
Blame Bartles.
Blame James.
They make alcohol that tastes like Kool Aid
Hey Kool Aid! Oh yeah!
You said, mimicking the fat red pitcher we all came to love as a child
You kissed me hard and pushed me by my face
Out of my way it's my night sucka'
I played host
To thirty of our closest friends
While you inflicted love and destruction upon everything in your path
Like a beautiful Bridezilla
Later that night
I saw you standing on the balcony alone
You were laughing
I put my arms around you and whispered in your ear
My wife
It was the first time I had said those words in my life
Why are you laughing?
You leaned back on me and said
I've been lifting my gown
And showing my panties
To everyone that walks by
It's funny...
I'm sleepy...
Take me to bed
I carried you to our room
And you collapsed face down
Onto our bed
With and without grace
The most beautifully clumsy pile of lace
The world would ever know

Karma

Writing a poem
In my wife's office on a Saturday afternoon
While she caught up on paperwork,
She looked up from her desk
Just long enough to ask me
Can you help me with a project?
No, I replied,
I'm writing a poem.
She stormed off
Instantly I realized
The error in my math
Wife is never equal to, never less than,
But always greater than *poem*
I asked her what she needed help with
Nothing!
Go write your stupid little poem!
A half an hour later
I apologized
She rolled her eyes
And half smiled
In that I could care less sort of way that she does
When I know she has forgiven me
Even when she doesn't want to
I reached into the candy jar on her desk
Pulled out a snack size Mr. Goodbar
There wasn't anything good about it
I accidentally swallowed it whole
It lodged in my throat for what may have been one second
Or an eternity
I'm not sure
She looked up to God
Deliberately excluding me from the conversation and said,
Thank you...
Having just nearly escaped death
Wiping watery eyes
I coughed up a one-word reply,
...Really?
What...
She replied pointing to the sky,
She gets me.

Lost and Found

1.

The Waitress at the Local Diner

My father found me
My father found me after ten years
My father found me on Facebook
It has been ten years since he left me
And my mother
I was eight
He was twenty-eight
I gladly accepted him as my friend
I do not know if my mother will like this
I looked through all of his photos late last night
He has two sons with another woman
She looks younger than him
I do not know if she will like this
The youngest son looks just like me
My father found me on Facebook
I gladly accepted him as my friend
I do not know if I can accept him as anything else

2.

The Father of the Waitress at the Local Diner

I found my daughter
I found my daughter that I abandoned
I found her on Facebook
She accepted me
It was three hours and fourteen minutes after I sent the request
Or rather it was ten years three hours and fourteen minutes after I sent the request
I do not know if it was hesitantly
Or reluctantly
Or begrudgingly
But she accepted me
I looked through all of her photos late last night
She looks like her mother
She looks tired and beautiful
And more than a little sad
She is a waitress in a small diner
She attends night school at a community college
She has a boyfriend
He looks older than she does
What happens next
What will I be to her

An occasional comment under a photo
A caption
A response
A semi colon followed by a close parenthesis
I do not know if she will ever accept me as anything more
Than an emoticon

3.

The Mother of the Waitress at the Local Diner

My daughter found her father
Or rather he found her
On Facebook
Of all places
And she
Accepted him
It wasn't hard to figure out her password
Single mothers know all of their daughters' secrets
Even the ones they think we don't know
I looked through all of his photos late last night
He looks ridiculous
Stupid
And more than a little happy
I hate him for that
I hate him for leaving her
But I hate him more for finding her
My daughter is a waitress
And a student
She has a boyfriend
He is the exact same age her father was when he left her
What is it about fatherless women and older men
What is it about the fathers who abandon them
Maybe it all comes down to acceptance and denial
The mother in me can accept this for what it is
Just another case of lost and found
The woman in me will never accept any of it

I'll Never Forget

I'll never forget
The day
My three-year old daughter
Walked into my bathroom
Without knocking
Door mistakenly unlocked
To find me standing in front of the toilet...
Peeing—
I shouted
Something involving the words
Mi'ja...
Please...
Don't...
Look...
It was only a brief moment
Perhaps nothing more than a second or two
Her head tilted to one side
The way she does
When she explores something new
Something foreign to her
Then as I stumbled
Angling myself away from her puzzled gaze
Reaching for my zipper
Peeing a bit on my shoe
Desperate to cover the part of me
A daughter should never see
I saw it slowly creep over her face
Fear
Ungodly
Unspeakable fear
Of something she couldn't begin to fathom
She turned and ran wildly
Arms flinging
Voice screaming loudly
Her shrieks of terror filled our home
I'll never forget
Those words
They haunt me to this day
Daddy's got doo doo in the front!
Daddy's got doo doo in the front!
Daddy's got doo doo in the front!

HOPE
5 MILES

The last sign I remember reading
before I pulled into the rest stop read
HOPE 5 MILES
I noticed a large black man
enter the restroom just before me
a skinny white teenager
entered just after me.
There were just three stalls.
And there we all sat
like the worst Benetton colors of the world clothing advertisement ever created.
I normally don't like stall talk,
but I couldn't resist,
I said,
"You know King dreamed that someday
little black boys and little white boys and little brown boys
would all stand side by side holding hands.
Well, at least we're all…
you know…
sitting
side by side.
That's a pretty good start."
They laughed.
I laughed.
We all laughed
like wild eyed boys who measured themselves
by single parents and bruises and curse words and laughter
but never by color.
Maybe hope was closer than I thought.

Final Exam for My Father

1. True or False. The night that you walked out me and my mother, you hesitated before grabbing the doorknob.

2. If a bus leaves the city at 60 miles per hour to nowhere in particular, and a man on that bus has left his only son behind in the darkness of that city, how many miles will it take before that son forgets what his father's hands look and feel like?

3. On the night that you left us, how many hearts did you break?

    A. one, mine
    B. one, my mother's
    C. two, mine and my mother's
    D. three, mine, my mother's and yours

4. True or False. In certain species of the animal kingdom, when a male member of that species abandons his offspring that male member of that species is ostracized, beaten, and in some instances killed.

5. In the space provided, define the terms further, farther, and father.

6. On the night that your father died, what if anything did you have to say to God?

7. When we survived nine days in a row before the welfare check came in, on a bag of maiz and a crock pot full of wishes that tasted just like frijoles, did you feel the fire on your fingertips every time my mother winced as she turned the tortilla on the open flame?

8. Because of your blood, I have spent every day of my life enveloped by skin that's too light to be brown and too dark to be white. I used to hate this about myself, but I have finally come to love this about myself. What do you love and hate about yourself?

9. As a young man you

    A. never loved a young, beautiful dark brown woman.
    B. loved one young, beautiful dark brown woman.
    C. loved many young, beautiful dark brown women
    D. loved only the idea of young beautiful dark brown women

10. List five things that you are truly grateful for and five things that you are truly regretful for.

11. A famous American poet's mother once said, "[Single] mothers are almost always better men than men are." What do you make of this?

12. Without using the words, "I'm" or "sorry" in the space provided write an apology letter to my mother.

13. On a scale from one to ten, with one being not difficult at all and ten being quite difficult, how challenging do you think it is for a guerro to grow up in the barrio of the lower east side?

14. As a child your son remembers hearing his drunk uncles whisper in hushed voices not meant for his ears that more than likely you were not that child's father. What if anything do you have to say to them?

15. Finish this sentence:

My son, if I only had one thing to say to you, it would be

And one final question to conclude the test:

Would it mend or break your heart if I told you,

I forgive you?

Reinventing the Enemy's Language

On November 29, 1864, a three-year-old Apache child
Stood on the banks of the Sand Creek looking up to the sky.
Three US Calvary soldiers 75 feet away used him for target practice.
The third shot found its mark.

So much more than Christopher Columbus has come between us
The conqueror and the conquered
So for crimes against defenseless children
There will always be a space between us
There can be no *we*
I have cut that word out of me
The way one removes a tumor
Not as an act of desperation
But rather an act of necessity
I've read too many books to believe what they tell me
There was no glory in any of this
But there were piles of lifeless children
Cast aside like unwanted dolls
Whose only crime was being born with skin the color of earth
So with this poem,
I reinvent the enemy's language
Blanket shall no longer mean small pox
But rather warmth
Blood will symbolize sacrifice not death
Corpse will be pronounced chrysalis
And under the sky of the once Great Plains
Bullets through the process of metamorphosis
Will transform before our very eyes
Into giant monarch butterflies
Crawling from the inward out of a heart
Of a three-year-old child with skin akin to the life-giving color of dirt
So skin will come to mean begin
And heart will become synonymous for start
Because his death is the beginning
Of the reinventing of the enemy's language
Trail will simply mean path, not tears
1492 will be nothing more than a year
That came and went
Just like all the others
The arms and legs of children hacked into bite-sized portions for dog feed
Will be sewn back together into wings
That spread like dreams of a heaven where children
Rest in peace not pieces
Drums will signify dance not war
Buffalo will run and children will soar
Like giant monarch butterflies

Over Plains that will once again be Great
My love for you mutates to hate
As you force me to see you slit my daughter's throat
And I watch the blood flow out of her like hope
And because of that there is no more love in me to give
Because of that I take the word, forgive
And from this day forward it shall mean redeem
Because some crimes are unforgivable
The way some lives are barely livable
And as I kneel by my lifeless child
I find myself surrounded by all the percussive forces of a small o
The metallic ring behind me
The open mouth beneath me
One an ending, one a beginning
And my last words in this existence will be,

Taku
Waon kowokipi sni

Whatever you do to hurt me
Is not enough to make me fear you

And one day many years from now
A new child will be born
With skin the color of earth
And a voice that soars like giant monarch butterflies at sunrise
And for no reason at all she will come up to you
She will embrace you and she will whisper in your ear

_{Will you help me reinvent the enemy's language?}
_{Will you help me reinvent the enemy's language?}
Will you help me reinvent the enemy's language?

You will not recognize her face
But you will recognize her scar
And you will look at her the way a child looks up to the sky
Because he's closer to God than we are
And you will take her hand gently in yours

And you will say,

Yes

Tag...

for Aida

My father never touched me
While your father touched you too much
And such is life
We're all just little wooden pegs
Inside plastic cars
Doing the best we can to hide our scars
While God's hand is at the wheel
Dictating the way we feel
We spent our childhood playing hide and seek
In a city so big
That the meek didn't have a chance to inherit happiness
Let alone the world
And this is how it was for a lost boy and a sad girl
We were always just around the corner from one another
I think my cousin knew your brother
There was always something between us
Some weird coincidence or another
Like God was screaming down from heaven
What do I have to do to get you two together?
We were birds of a feather on opposite sides of the flock
Street kids who grew up on opposite ends of the same block
All the while me not realizing
That somewhere near the end of Bonita Blvd
There was someone pretty waiting for me to find her
Life is funny that way
It took me 18 years to find you
20 more to carve out a life with you
And two daughters, two degrees, one mortgage, one dog,
One hundred Dominoes pizzas,
And more poems than I can imagine later
I just wanted to take one moment out of this crazy ride called life to tell you

Thank you

Thank you for finding me

Thank you for your loud laugh
And your crooked smile
Thank you for the way you looked at our daughter last night
As you held her in your arms
Daring the world to try and bring her harm
"I wish a mother falcon would try and hurt my baby..."
Thank you for all the times you searched
And all the times you hid

Thank you for being the street kid,
The sad girl that hid from me
In an 18 year game of hide and seek
Thank you for this life you've given me,
Every single bit
The game isn't over
It's just begun
Tag…you're it.

Cumbersome

The beautiful dark skinned woman at Gate 18
Was definitely an islander
All cheek bones and flowing hair
Long and dark as runway asphalt
The daughters that stepped off the plane into her arms
Were mestizos like me
Mixed blood
White father/brown mother
The mother
Their mother
Wept at their return
The way one weeps at extreme moments of joy or distress
It could have been the joy of their return
Or the distress of them loving their father and his new wife
His new life
More than the life they had briefly left behind
The mother held them close as they walked away
So close it became cumbersome for them to walk
The mother had words tattooed on each wrist
I wanted to believe they were the names of the daughters
But I was too far from the scene to be certain
I wanted to believe that the daughters returned gladly
That they wished to never visit their father and his new family again
But I knew I was projecting
Their father could have been a kind and just man
Who simply fell out of love with the beautiful dark skinned woman,
Who wished to remain friends
And share equally in the job of raising the daughters
But her tears
Reminded me of my mother sobbing late at night

When she thought I was asleep
When she thought I wouldn't hear
And I know now that many of those tears
Fell at the thought of my father
And many fell at the thought of me
Looking so much like him

By the Numbers

1

I was the one thing my mother and father had in common
A man and woman different as conqueror and conquered
Different as war and peace
I always see them as this metaphor
But what does that make me
Am I the land over which the war was waged
Am I the possibility of all that is to come
Am I water and mineral rights
Am I the gentrification of their souls
No, I am the peace treaty that both sides broke

2

I like to imagine it happened at 2:00 AM
All acts of recklessness
Happen at such ungodly hours
Question:
What do you get
When you combine
The back seat of a Chevy Nova
With the sweat
Of two young, stupid, beautiful people
And Marvin Gaye's voice on the radio?
Answer:
Me

3

My mother had three sons from three different men
So we all look different
And the same

4

I must have been four years old
The year my brother Mauricio was born
All flesh and appetite
We called him Gordo
Some still do
That year my mother gave him to my aunt to raise
But he knew/knows/always will know
That he is my brother

5

When my youngest brother Cristobal turned five
I left home for good
I was a teenager
With what my mother called a mouth on him
I have yet to forgive myself
For leaving something so small and beautiful
Behind in the darkness of my youth

6

I have been told on six different occasions
That I look like my grandfather
Who raised me when my mother could not
And my father would not
Six people have said I look like my grandfather,
Who taught me everything I know about life, love, poetry,
and what it is to be a good man
I remember every instance when someone has said this to me
The first was my mother
The last was my wife

7

Do you know why seven is everyone's favorite number? It's because seven is the combination of the archetypal numbers three and four. Three is a masculine number; think the Holy Trinity. Four is a feminine number; think the life cycle and the four seasons. Seven is the possibility of harmony between man and woman. Seven is balance and order. Seven is perfection. But I never cared for the number, because when I learned this, I immediately associated seven with my mother and father. To me, seven, like my mother and my father, is just another odd thing.

8

There were eight of us
The vato locos
Who would run wildly
Through the barrio streets of my youth
They weren't bad boys
They were boys who sometimes did bad things
They were more than friends
They were my brothers
All of them
Over the years I've lost touch with them
I'm not sure if they all made it out of the barrio
I am sure that a few didn't

I remember once I asked Jesús
Where do you want to live when you grow up?
He didn't answer so I asked again
Hey vato, where do you see yourself when you're 30?
I'll never make it to 30
I remember laughing it off and cursing at him in Spanglish
But both he and I knew
That there was a good chance
That what he said would come true
Whether or not it did is my own private poem
That I'm not ready to tell

9

There were nine of them,
Including my tío Silastino,
Who was the biggest and strongest of all my uncles,
And the only one to never marry and have children of his own.
When he died a slow agonizing death from cancer
He left me a sum of money.
He looked out for me because
Of all of his nieces and nephews
I was the only one being raised by a single mother,
So he showered me with gifts at birthdays and Christmases.
And with his last will and testament
He wanted to give me one last present,
But days before his death
His eight brothers and sisters
Including my mother
Finding their brother to be of unfit mind and body
Changed the will
And the money that was to go to me went instead to them
And rightfully so
They were the ones after all caring for him those last hard months.
I didn't find out about this until years after the fact
When my mother confessed it to me.
I would have given the money gladly,
It wasn't what was done
But rather how it was done.
And I knew
At that moment
That they always belonged to me,
But I never belonged to them.

10

I was the one thing my mother and father had in common, born from an act of recklessness. One of those beautiful mistakes they don't like to talk about at parties.

Years later on her deathbed if she asks me, what do you remember most about your family? I will answer, that we all look different and the same. Maybe my birth all comes down to flesh and appetite. Have they yet to forgive themselves for their hunger? Do you remember every instance in which someone has said I love you? If you're lucky one of seven men or women who said it, actually meant it. Maybe every answer to every question lies in a private poem you're not ready to tell, one that describes a slow agonizing hell. A poem that belongs to you but that you never belong to.

Another Kind of Graveyard

Once while driving home
From a graveyard shift
Tired and bewildered by life
Much too fatigued to react
With any sense of quickness or alertness
I ran over a black and white kitten
That darted out in front of me
I pulled over
Walked back to the mangled body
Broken in so many places
But despite all that metal
All that weight
All that gravity
Despite all of Newton's laws
And Darwin's theories
The kitten cried
It did not meow
But rather it cried like a child might
That had been broken in so many places and left to die
I picked up the mangled creature
And walked across the street to an inner city park
Laid the poor kitten
Still wailing in agony under the shade of a live oak
Then with one swift movement
I snapped its neck under the heel of my shoe
I did so without looking
Which was cowardly
I turned away and stood there in the silence and death of it all
I walked back to my car and drove the rest of the way home
The next morning
I noticed the blood on my sole
I picked the shoes up and threw them one at a time
Across the room
Into the trash
I have never told another living soul
But I think of it often
The poem is my confession
The page my religion
The noun the slain son
The adjective the ghost
The verb is God
And I am just another sinner
With blood on his hands

Clean

for my father

"Before you embark on a journey of revenge, dig two graves."
        -Confucius

I thought I was digging one grave
But I was digging two
One for me
One for you
I spent years in the dark
Just another kind of setting son
I guess some things can't be undone
So I claw at the dirt
Fight my way to the light
Tell myself everything will be all right
If I just keep climbing
I've grown filthy it's true
The dirt under my nails
Is the last part of you
So I climb from this grave
Try and wash you away
But you always find a way to stay
The memory of you lingers
Like the smell of damp earth
Or the sight of a funeral hearse
So I grab my spade
Slam it into the piles I've made
Filling both holes with dirt, sweat, and tears
Feeling whole for the first time in years
I drop to my knees
Lift my arms to the rain
Let my true Father wash away the pain
And find a way to forgive you
Despite the fact that you hurt me
Despite the fact that I'm dirty
Don't you see what I mean?
Sometimes it's when you're at your filthiest
That you feel most clean

House Fires

The house still stands erect to this day
But my family burned down long ago
My mother dispersed as ashes
Scattered about at a moment's whim
Caught beneath the boot soles and fingernails of men
Who would brush her away when she tried so desperately to cling to them
To cling to anything
My father who was always nothing more than smoke
Remained in this gaseous state before, during, and after the fire expired
To calm the flames we shattered every window in the house
So he never lingered the way smoke tends to
But rather he drifted coolly out of our lives as he was always want to do
I remember as a child trying desperately to hold smoke in my hands
But some things exist for the sole purpose of leaving
They are always leaving
The ember that was my brother glows faintly
Like a dying celestial body
Leaving only traceries of its once vibrant brilliance
And like a child praying before a votive candle
In the shadows of a cathedral
I find myself breathing on the ember that was once a fire
Hoping
Praying for the smallest spark
To shatter the darkness
They say some children are born of fire, smoke and ash
I was one such child
I always belonged to the flame
But it never belonged to me
I tried so hard to extinguish it
To put it behind me
But some fires burn too deeply

For the Jewel Thieves

[she] was not the diamond
nor the coal
but the diamond mine

      -natasha carrizosa

When our time here is done,
Let them say that we lived our lives
The way young mothers
Who were hurt deeply by their fathers
Protect their sons and daughters,
With unforgiving, reckless abandon.
When our time is here is done
And we look back at our footprints in the sand
At all those times when there were not two sets but one
We'll tell them, those are the times we carried our God with us
Let them say I remember his sad eyes and her beautiful smile
All the while,
Knowing that it was our curse word for the world ways that made them love us
Let them say we were storytellers
Caught somewhere between a lie and the truth
Like a lost child seeking refuge from her youth
My father's fingers and tongue ruined my manners toward God
I stood in the rain for hours once trying to wash him off of me
You said this to me
So let this be the defining image
When we are but a memory
Let our words fall on you like a cold, hard rain
Incessantly
The clearest water falling from the darkest sky
Casting off the when and where
While clinging to the why
Let them say
He was a jewel thief
And she was a diamond mine
He stole the most radiant pieces of her
And placed them in his poems without asking
This is what I remember about him
How he was sometimes hurtful and ugly
Though he tried not to be
How his words were lovely
But never as beautiful as her eyes
Let them say that we lived
Every second like it was our last
How we mined the souls of the people we loved
Sifting though a past

Long since forgotten
To find that elusive poem that may or may not change the world
Because this is all we ever truly knew how to do

Just After Night Falls

It happens just after night falls
As a waiter waits his tables
As an actor's curtain calls
We all fall victim to the beauty of the night
Like we never felt so clean
As when we stood under a lamppost's gleam
And somewhere in the middle of nowhere America
At midnight
In the children's ward
In a hospital bed
A mother envelops her dying child
From her pajama covered feet to her balding head
Trying to love her daughter back to life
It's the reason dreamers choose to rest
And poets choose to write
Because we both know the best time to lie is at night
And somewhere in an alley near the theater district
A junkie is startled by the sound of applause
Just long enough for a momentary pause
As he notices that his track mark scars
Are mirror images of the nighttime's stars
This is where his life begins and ends
Somewhere between a flesh carved Pleiades
And his mother's softly whispered *please*
It happens just after night falls
Somewhere between the pimp's street
And the cop's beat
Two awkward teenage lovers
Will realize that even without the engine running
There's enough heat in that back seat for the both of them
It's the arsonist counting to ten before he throws the match
It's a woman's hand trembling as she triple locks the latch
After night falls
We all become just a little bit more alive
And a little less clean
We all have to struggle a little bit harder to be seen
Like we were all characters in a novel by Richard Wright
And in the middle of the night
In Lashkar Gah Afghanistan
A man
Desperately awaits the light
As he prepares the bomb
That will take his life
And eleven others
So thank God for the darkness
It's the time we all look most like brothers

It's the music of a playwright's typewriter bouncing off his apartment walls
As death is being sold in nearby tenement halls
It's the reason rainfall and kick ball
Both feel better just after night falls
So stand on that sidewalk
Like you were the brightest diamond in the jewelry store case
And shine
Let the moonlight fall on you like your lover's arms
And embrace the night
Like it was your last
Because at night
There is no past
There is only the living moment
We are all shooting stars
Flashing across the night sky
Some burn brighter than others
Some crash to earth too soon
But all of you
Every single one of you
Has the power to be one of Kerouac's
spider of fireworks exploding in the night sky
So don't befall to nights of quiet desperation
Because somewhere between the street kids' game of nighttime football
And the Lower East Side bar hopper's catcall
In a coffee shop sits two young strangers
Who give each other a sideways look
Because they are both reading the same book
One of those simple and tragic stories by Paulo Coelho
Where everything depends on chance and night
Like two strangers sitting in a coffee shop
Who don't know that they will be lovers soon
Like two flowers blossoming by the light of the full moon
It doesn't happen like this for all
But it happens for some
Just after night falls

Flawed

for my wife

She said,
Don't love me
I'm flawed.
I've got more scars
Than the night's got stars
And if you get any closer to me
You'll learn the reason I'm so wild
Is because my father's fingers and tongue
Ruined my manners toward men as a child
You'd realize the only reason I'm flirty
Is to disguise the fact that you're clean and I'm dirty.
And I don't share my pain with God
So what makes you think I'll share it with you

And I look her in the eyes
And I say
I choose you
I choose the possibility of us
I choose the way you smile when I cuss
Over something as simple as forgetting a line to a poem
I choose our someday daughter
And the way I know you'll hold her
Like she was the baptism that would cleanse you of all this strife
So I bartered a scholarship
For the chance to see what our love could teach us about life
And don't ask me about regret
Regret is a poem I haven't written yet.
I choose you
I choose us
So when you push
I pull
And I don't begrudge the fact
That you only learned the first half of the golden rule
Do unto others
Before they do unto you
And it's true
Keeping people at arm's length
Means they can't touch you
So I earn your trust
The way children trace the lines in the coloring book
With slow deliberate movements
Always asking before touching
And still you flinch
Like the memory of your father's lust

Was a barbed wire fence
Covered in rust
But your laugh is like a pair of wire cutters
So every chance I get
I tell you a bad joke, like…
What does a nosy pepper do?
Gets *JALAPEÑO* business!
And you smile
Knowing all the while that I can't write your nightmares away
So I watch you sleep
And when your eyes begin to sway
In that frightful kind of way
I softly jostle you and say
You're safe
You're okay
And I watch you drift off into sleep
I don't bother asking God for your soul to keep
Because I know a few things to be true
Like I know God is in you
I know the reason you're afraid of a doctor's needle
I know angels walk among us disguised as people
I know I told you once you were the kind of woman I could easily fall in love with
I did
I am
Not despite your flaws
But because of them

Negative

I remember the first time I saw Manny shoot someone
It was as though he carried a piece of all of his victims around with him
Their statuesque faces frozen
Motionless for all time
I remember the first time Manny shot me
Standing outside Roy Hernandez' Barbershop
Broom in hand
Caught with my head down
Gazing at the myriad of cracks that lined this particular sidewalk
In this particular barrio
Marveling over the countless backs of mothers broken
By the ambivalent footsteps of careless children
When the flash rang out
Brooding brown eyes blinded by the light
Then the recoil of a spring mechanism
A soft grinding sound
And there Manny stood
Fanning himself
Polaroid in hand
Slowly the image began to appear
Me in the foreground
The street sign behind me read Bonita Boulevard
But there wasn't anything pretty about it
He showed me the photo but wouldn't let me hold it
And rightfully so
It was his image
It was his magic
I remember he said to me,
Damn vato, you look lost in thought
Maybe we were all lost back then
Maybe we were all waiting to be someone's victim

Maybe we were all waiting for someone with magic in his hands
To show us we were beautiful

Incongruent

When you ask me,
What tribe are you?
I can tell you what you want to hear.
On my mother's side I am Sioux.
That way you can associate me with
The medicine woman
The feather in her hair and not the spear in her hand.
You can admire us both
For our connection to the earth
And the four sacred directions that frame it.
Or I can tell you what you don't want to hear.
On my father's side I am Apache.
And my stoic eyes force you to see me as the warrior that I am.
My spirit is a horse
Wild and unbroken
And although I extend my arm to shake your hand
You know that more than anything
I want to see your blood dripping from my blade.
Or I can tell you the truth,
That my father's grandfather's grandfather was Wichita
That I am separated from him by seven generations
That it has taken me 175 years to find him
That I have gone most of my life without any knowledge of his existence
That the fraction of him that makes up my blood is so far from being whole
That I wonder if he knew then
What I know now
Would he lay with that white woman
Love her, in spite of her alabaster flesh
Or when for the first time
His dark, brooding eyes met her eyes blue as sky
Would he simply turn and walk away

It Happens By Fractions

Whole
One-Half
One-Fourth
One-Eighth
One-Sixteenth

Her heart has been broken in half
by men who used their beautifully stunning eyes
to hide their beautifully cunning lies
and I wonder
how many times can a heart break
in two
before it is too fractured
to be broken
or for that matter
mended
again.

One-Thirty-Second
One Sixty-Fourth
One Hundred Twenty-Eighth…

Forgetting Jude

I remember I spilled white rice on the kitchen floor as a child.
My mother looked up from the sopa.
Red as blood she was stirring on the kitchen stove.
Then she turned,
slowly walked out of the room and returned
with a large print
hardbound copy of the family Bible
that contained both testaments—
in Spanish and English.
She had me kneel on the rice
handed me the Bible
and then returned to stirring the sopa.
You may rise,
if you can name all twelve apostles.
She had her back to me,
but I could tell she was crying.

Peter,

his brother (Andrew),

the two Jameses,

Judas,

John,

Phillip,

Thomas,

Matthew,

Alph...ee...us?

Simon.

Then silence.

I watched the clock, and not her,
as I struggled for the name that escaped me.
It was just under 12 minutes,
one for each disciple.
Then she said,
Get up and take that Bible back to the altar in the sala.
I went to the bathroom
and washed the blood off my knees,
marveling how it was the weight of my flesh,
the weight of the Word
that did this to me.
I washed my face hard with cold water,
stared at the mirror in front of me
and noticed for the first time
how much lighter my skin was than my mother's.
Did she hurt me for all the white men who'd ever hurt her?
All of this was suppose to teach me to be careful not to spill.
All of this was suppose to teach me discipline.
All of this was suppose to teach me right from wrong.
But all I learned
from those cuts on my knees,
from the weight of that Bible,
from those 12 minutes
was that gravity hurts.

It Ends the Way It Begins

When I tell people I'm a poet
They inevitably ask
What does that mean
And I say what do you mean,
What does that mean
And they say
*I mean writing poetry is very Renaissance of you
But how do you make your living?
What is it that you actually do?*
And I say,
I remind the world
That a woman as black as night
Carried a child the color of alabaster
Away from a hurricane
Named after a Russian woman
It happened at night
In the middle of a city-wide blackout
So if you were there
Walking across the bridge with them
You couldn't tell
Where black flesh ended
And white skin began
Unless you extended your hand
To touch them.
This is what I do
I find the poetry in simple things
Something as ordinary and common as the color blue
And I spit it out on stage for you
You know the ancient Greeks had no word for blue
So Homer referred to the sea as wine dark
As if any ark that traveled it waves
Bobbled about like a drunken man
Reaching out for a nonexistent hand
You see this is how the poem begins
It just weaves its way in
The way blue thread weaves its way into Old Glory
Now there's a story
Did you know 150 years ago Captain William Driver,
Who coined the phrase Old Glory,
Had his flag sewn into the middle of his neighbor's daughter's blanket
Hiding it like it was a Jewish boy engulfed by Holocaust
Who would someday write poems about survival and forgiveness
And during the Civil War when a Confederate flag flew
A little girl in Tennessee was tucked in every night in red, white and blue
And it's true
And fitting that blue means perseverance

We've become practiced in this kind of blue
Me
You
A single mother
A homeless white boy
A Black President
We all hide things to keep them safe
We all wrap ourselves in the things we believe in
I once saw a homeless man rip the pages from a book
Skipping over certain passages
Deliberate in the ones he took
He stuffed them in his coat to keep him warm
Using words to weather the storm
You see this is what I do
I use lines of poetry to weather the storm in me
Like metaphor is a buoy
In the middle of the darkest sea
So dark it's more akin to black than blue
I point out things like this to you
I write poems that like all moons yearn to be blue
Not because they're beautiful
But because they're rare
As rare and as brilliant
As you
And this is how the poem ends
The same way that it begins
With blue ink scribbled across a page
As I stand on a small wooden stage
Asking you
To let my words
Be the fleshy arms that carry you away from the storm
Away from the night
Away from black
And away from white
Just long enough to remind you
That storm clouds like most people's faith
Are not strong enough to endure the returning Son
And the only things I know to be true
Is that storm clouds like hate are temporary
Poetry like love is immortal
And the darkest sky will always return to blue

Mix Tape Biographical Sonnet (Joaquín Zihuatanejo)

1. Mellon Collie and the Infinite Sadness by Smashing Pumpkins
2. Son's Gonna Rise by Citizen Cope
3. Building Steam With a Grain of Salt by DJ Shadow
4. Despedida by Shakira
5. Happy Birthday to Me (Feb 15) by Bright Eyes
6. Alive by Pearl Jam
7. Where Have You Been by Manchester Orchestra
8. Such Great Heights by Iron & Wine

9. Undenied by Portishead
10. Unravel by Björk
11. A Rush of Blood to the Head by Coldplay
12. All I Need by Radiohead

13. End of the Day by Beck
14. We'll Meet Again by Johnny Cash

Mix Tape Biographical Sonnet (Aída Zihuatanejo)

in no particular order

God Moving Over The Face of the Waters by Moby
Analyse by Thom Yorke
Unravel by Björk
Someone Saved My Life Tonight by Elton John
To Know Him Is to Love Him by Amy Winehouse
Bound to You by Christina Aguilera
Adagio for TRON by Daft Punk
Airplane Mode by Flobots
Right Where It Belongs by Nine Inch Nails
A Place Called Home by PJ Harvey
Something Beautiful by Sinead O'Connor
Breathe Me by Sia
Ode to My Family by The Cranberries
The Unforgettable Fire by U2

Mix Tape Biographical Sonnet (Aiyana Marisol Zihuatanejo)

1. Those to Come by The Shins
2. Tamer Animals by Other Lives
3. Paper Aeroplane by Angus & Julia Stone
4. House of Cards by Vitamin String Quartet
5. Houdini (Acoustic) by Foster the People
6. Heavy Rope by LIGHTS
7. Bonfire by Childish Gambino
8. So This Is Goodbye (Pink Ganter Remix) by William Fitzsimmons

9. You're a Wolf by Sea Wolf
10. Clementine by Sarah Jaffe
11. No Church in the Wild by Jay Z, Kanye West, The-Dream, Frank Ocean
12. Alive with the Glory of Love by Say Anything

13. Up Against the Wall by Peter, Bjorn & John
14. Good So Far by Mackintosh Braun

Mix Tape Biographical Sonnet (Dakota Salis Zihuatanejo)

1. Brick By Boring Brick By Paramore
2. Better by Regina Spektor
3. I Like Giants by Kimya Dawson
4. Human Behavior by Björk
5. Bitter by Teddy Geiger
6. I'm Not Okay (I Promise) by My Chemical Romance
7. Sweet Dreams (Are Made of This) by Eurythmics
8. I Was Born (A Unicorn) by The Unicorns

9. Secrets Don't Make Friends by Rocky Loves Emily
10. Yeah 3X by Chris Brown
11. Bigcitydreams by Never Shout Never
12. The One That Got Away by Katy Perry

13. Fix You by Coldplay
14. All These Things That I've Done by The Killers

Abuelo

He placed tomato
In my palm, surely he placed
His heart there as well

Mother

Her cheekbones like moons
Still orbit through memories
They follow me still

Father

It's time I give up
The weight of you, and carry
You no more. Goodbye.

Aída

I will gladly sit
Under the shade tree and read
And swing beside you

Aiyana

Bottled water
Cheese
High Fiber Bread
Needle
Insulin
Daughter's lunch

Dakota

I know now you are
More your mother than me
Lovely geometry

Summer

for my daughters and the mocosos from Barrio East Side

gold honey suckle
between children's lips—niños—
savor this season

'mana (recipe for a poet)

sangre:

one half poet
on mother's side/one half warrior
on father's

los muchachos perdidos (The Lost Boys)

I owe you all
So much more than metaphor,
More than just ink on page.

la familia de mi juventud (The Family of My Youth)

You were the split tree
I was the metal ring
My fragile family

Students

Homework:

1. Read
2. Write
3. Repeat

My greatest lesson plan to date

Metaphorically Speaking

I will only write metaphor I've felt before
and simile must reveal what's real in me
and concerning hyperbole
exaggeration for effect is like the plague to me
because clarity only happens when you dare to see
the actual in you…the factual in me
you
me
we
two
become one
through this poem
which makes you and I
us
and the dichotomy in me
will divide me
but not conquer me
because I believe my mother's dream lives in me
and although my father existed only in the occasional child support check
and the even less occasional phone call
my childhood was anything but a no man's land
I prayed to the same moon my Abuelo planted under
I cursed the sun that my tíos toiled under
and somehow I managed to bloom
but it was the life giving roots that made all the difference
and I grew best in the muck and mire-filled ditches of my youth
so thank you Barrio East Side
thank you Abuelo
thank you tíos
y tías
thank you mamá
and thank you father
it is true
I am the sunflower
growing wildly in the alley
adjacent to nothing
that Jesús Santos pointed out to me
when we were no longer children and not yet men
and my arms are petals
reaching out to Aztlán
and someday I will reach it
and you must know
when that day comes
I will take you with me

Perfection from Flaw

When I want something to come to pass
I ask my daughters to pray for it
You see, I believe
that since women and God
are the only two things that can create life
women are more closely linked to God than men.
Women are a reflection of the divine in God,
the love, the benevolence, the strength
where as we are a manifestation of God's shadow
the anger, the wrath, the fury.
As a child in the church that was named for Her
I found myself praying to La Virgen de Guadalupe
more than the Man on the cross,
in His eyes I saw the reflection
of the pain and rage I felt for my father
Father, why have you forsaken me?
But in the eyes of the Virgin I saw salvation
I thought if I prayed hard enough
She could go to the powerful Father
and the slain Son
and intercede on my behalf
the blue paint on her gown chipped away in some places
revealing the pure white plaster beneath
perfection made evident by flaw

Scarlet Poem

for Aída,
I'll always be the Dimmesdale to your Hester
the Peeta to your Katniss
because it was you
who saved me

it was Hawthorne who wrote in his scarlet novel
the coming savior of our time must be a woman
a woman steeped in sacrifice, strength, and selflessness
so while many find themselves waiting for the son
to return and redeem us all
I wait for the daughter to come
in human form
among us,
and she will come
and she will save us,
she will save us all

Slow Down, 'Manito

He was such an odd boy from the barrio,
so white and speaking Spanish,
always running, a blur of speed.
He ran from the moon
and the sun,
from the night
and the day,
ran from our dark, scared mestiza of a mother
and his shadow of a father
ran so as not to slow down
or God forbid ever stop
because if he did
he might realize that despite his beauty and innocence
he was alone.

And all I ever wanted to say was,
Slow down,
listen to the soft tones in your Abuelo's voice
therein lies your sanctuary
savor the aromas of la cocina on Sunday morning
luxuriate in the flavor of your people
let me read one of my books to you
there truly is magic in the words.

I want to say all this and more
but I don't
because I know he would just keep running
through the mean streets of our youth,
through the barrio,
through the pesadillas of my sleepless nights.

The best I can do
is to offer up a whisper
late at night
many years later
sitting in a chair that has scuffed the hardwood floors
I find myself whispering it more and more
as the years sprint by

Slow down,

slow down, 'manito.

My Tío Juan and His Way with Words

My tío Juan always had a way with words. Must have been the summer that followed fifth grade for me that my tío Juan turned to me and asked, "You ain't ever seen the Grand Canyon." My tío always asked questions like that, with declarative sentences.

"No," I replied.

"Ándale...we need to remedy that."

So the following weekend, he woke me up at 3:00 am and we made the drive from the barrio of East Dallas to Grand Canyon, Arizona. 16 hours by car, but my tío made it in a little over 15, I swear that man had a built in radar detector in his brain.

The drive was long and it was late so we pulled into a cheap motel for the night. I remember we ate burgers and fries as we watched a baseball game on a small television in the filthy room. The Yankees and someone but I don't remember who, but I know it wasn't our beloved Texas Rangers. I just remember my tío high-fiving me as the last pitch was thrown and the Yankees had lost a close one. "Remember, the close ones will always hurt you more." I remember he said that.

Between the motel, gasoline, and Dairy Queen we had already spent most of my tío's money, so we woke early, before sunlight, parked as far from the guarded gate as possible that blocked the entrance to the state park, and skirted our way alongside the far edge of the parking lot and managed to walk in without the guard so much as looking up from the paper he was reading.

We walked for what seemed like miles and followed the signs that eventually led us to a lookout. We waited in absolute silence for the sun to rise. Then, ever so slowly as though God himself was trying to tell us that beautiful things take time to bloom, the sun began to emerge over the horizon and illuminate a land filled with colors I had never seen. Shapes, textures, and depths I had never dreamed possible. I had never seen anything so beautiful and in a way so horrifying at the same time.

I remember we had just finished a lesson at the end of the school year on The Civil War. I seemed to recall reading something about it being the moment in history when our country's heart was broken. I remember thinking if something as big as a country has a heart and it breaks, then surely that fracture must look like this.

While all these thoughts ran through my mind, my tío Juan just stood there, rubbed his eyes for a bit, and then quietly with slow, deliberate movements as though he was in church or some place sacred he lit a cigarette, Marlboro I think, and smoked it almost all the way down to the filter. He dropped it on the ground and crushed it under his boot. And then after about five minutes of absolute silence, my tío turned to me and said something I'll never forget. He said, "Ándale...that is one big damn hole in the ground." Like I said, my tío Juan always had a way with words. And then he turned to me and said, "Well, I think we've seen all we can." We walked back to my tío's truck and drove from Grand Canyon, Arizona back home to the barrio of East Dallas. 16 hours by car, but my tío made it in a little under 15.

The Corner of Beautiful and Tomorrow

Thinking back on it now, I remember several things about that summer. I remember the heat, how it started early and lingered into the evening. It seemed to always be there that summer, waiting for us down at the neighborhood mercado. You could feel it radiating off of the unforgiving steel slide or iron monkey bars at the playground behind the barrio elementary school. Even on the corner of Bonita Blvd and Mañana Ave, which was our corner, it loitered, waiting for us.

You could carve the land that made up the earth into a million pieces but that corner, the corner of Bonita Blvd and Mañana Ave was our corner. We had claimed it for ourselves. Each one for his own reason. Some of us because we felt life owed us at least this simple span of concrete, asphalt and dirt. Some of us in the name of manifest destiny. Jesús Santos, vato loco with the holiest name on record, claimed it out of spite. Technically that cross section of broken sidewalk, the steps that led down to it, and the dirt that was gradually overtaking the last remnants of grass that made up the sad and pathetic front yard belonged to his mother and stepfather. Maybe it was the beatings he had endured at the hands of the drunken man that had married his mother two years earlier, or maybe it was for every time his mother would say something to him like, "Ay mijo you know he only gets like that when you make him mad, please mijo just leave him be tonight." Maybe it was just to piss them off, but he had claimed this corner at the beginning of the summer. We all had. And from that day on, it was our corner.

It was on this corner that I learned to curse and fight. I sat on this very curb as Manny passed me my first cigarette and laughed as I coughed violently after that first awkward toke. I laugh about it now because I was so scared of even the idea of addiction, that I just held the smoke in my mouth and did not inhale. But Jesús, Manny, Gustavo and the lot of them, they all inhaled deeply, holding the smoke in their lungs until they could no longer and it exploded from their mouths in short bursts of coughs followed by streams of translucence and consciousness. I don't think anyone in our gang cursed, or fought, or smoked for the conventional reasons, to feel good, to feel relaxed, to feel something. I think they all gave in to their vices to forget how lost they were. But then again we were all lost boys back then, caught somewhere between the light and the dark.

Manny, the atheist in the bunch had always believed that it was true what people said about us and people like us, poor, brown, young. "Damn vato, you got triple trouble!" Manny believed that we were all sinners in the hands of an angry God, so he turned his back on Him. Years later he would be shot dead by a Dallas Police Officer. Manny's life and death summed up concisely in a few sentences professionally stripped of adjectives on page 27A of The Dallas Times Herald. A few sentences. So much left out. So much left unsaid.

It seemed as though the entire world was losing touch with its humanity back then. Early in January that year Double Fantasy was the number one selling album in the world. I remember this well because a few weeks earlier Mark David Chapman accosted John Lennon outside his home, and asked him for an autograph. After Lennon signed a vinyl copy of Double Fantasy, the two exchanged smiles and pleasantries, and then Chapman shot and killed him. Reagan, the Pope, Sadat. They were all shot that year. Luckily for us, or so we foolishly thought in the states, it was Sadat who was successfully assassinated and not Reagan, so we all kept our eyes to the skies that year waiting for trickle down economics to trickle down on us. We're still waiting.

I also remember that one night. That dark, summer night that would divide my life into two parts, my childhood, which was more of a dream wandering than anything else, and every waking moment after it ended. I remember my tío Silastino, the biggest and strongest of all of my uncles waking me from a deep sleep.

"Mijo, get up! Get up now! I need you to run down the street to the mercado, to the pay phones there. Here's some change, call the police—911 send them to your tío Jose's house. Tell them there's been an accident, a horrible accident! But come directly home after. Do you here me? Come directly home. Go mijo, go now!"

"Sí tío."

It was the only time in my life I recall seeing him with tears streaming down his face, overcome with emotion, overcome by what the viejitos used to call la tristesa de la vida. It was the terror and pain in my tío's face that put the sense of urgency in me. I remember running the four blocks down Bonita Blvd, the feel of asphalt against bare feet. It was the only time that summer I recall feeling cold, running through dark barrio streets to a payphone that may or may not be out of order. Thinking back on it now, the barrio of my youth was always out of order. I know it was the fear in my tío's voice that caused me to cry as I pleaded with the emergency response operator to please send help quickly, but I don't know if it was courage or stupidity that took me to my tío Jose's house instead of the warmth of home.

I wasn't supposed to be there so I crept up slowly, cutting through yards, and staying close to the neighboring homes. I wanted to be just another shadow among the shadows. I did not think it was fair that I not know what was going on simply because I was a child. My tio Silastino and my tio Adolfo were there in front of the dark house on Jose's porch sharing an unfiltered Camel. I could hear the sirens of approaching emergency response vehicles, an ambulance, perhaps a fire truck. The police wouldn't be far behind. I crept to the side of the small, wood-frame house to the window that I knew would give me a view into the bedroom that my tío Jose and his beautiful wife Rosalinda shared. I peered in. I saw all. The blood. The knife. My tío in his rage. My lifeless tía on the floor in all her sadness and beauty. Mi Abuelo, my grandfather, standing between the two surrounded on both sides by the holocaust of it all.

It's funny, most people gradually grow into adulthood sometimes clinging tenaciously to their infancy. Others, the lost ones, have their innocence stripped from them at an early age, but for most, they struggle to find the point in their lives when they lost their innocence, when the simple beauty of youth began to elude them. I can tell you exactly when and how my childhood ended. It was the moment that I peered through that window, enveloped by the darkness of summer with the sound of sirens wailing in the distance.

Celestial Bodies

We look to our fathers
as the children of night look to the stars
our fathers, like stars
are distant
our fathers, like stars
are beautiful
our fathers, like stars
are unattainable.
The moment our childhood ends
is the moment we realize
that our fathers, like stars
died long before we came into existence,
and when we look at them
we see merely a reflection of what was once there.
As children we gladly barter illusion for the actual
we spend countless hours
coaxing our voices to shout
imploring our arms to reach out.
We seek the courage of the children of night
that spend a lifetime bellowing and grasping
for the smallest spark
anything to splinter the dark,
and to our fathers
who touched us inappropriately
or never touched us at all
who abandoned our mothers when they shouldn't have
or didn't abandon them when they should have
we must tell you now
that our arms are tired
and our voices are strained
and all we have left to offer you
is forgiveness.

About the Author

Joaquín Zihuatanejo is a husband/father/poet/teacher. Always in that order. He considers himself the Luther Vandross of the greater Dallas karaoke scene. He lost his first fistfight in second grade to a girl named Marcy Peavy. But in his defense she was stocky, and he had not yet seen The Karate Kid and thus had not yet been exposed to the paint the fence technique that would have proved beneficial in blocking her swift kick to the groin. He once played kickball in the rain for hours with a bunch of mocosos from the neighborhood. He counts this day as one of his best. He has been told by two Caucasians and three African Americans that he looks like he has a little Black in him. His daughter has been asked by one Mexican American and one white person, are you part Black? Which leads him to believe that he may have a little Black in him...he's not sure. He went to college and graduated with a BA in English. He is currently working on his MA in English. He hates English and thinks it is the most godforsaken language on the planet. As a teenager in the middle of a dark summer night, he once rode on the back of a moped with his friend Manny Valdez from Barrio East Side to downtown Dallas and back, all the while holding an am/fm cassette player boom box with graphic equalizer. The cassette in the tape deck was Escape by Journey. He had the volume turned all the way up. In 2006 he received a perfect score of 30 in the final round of the Individual World Poetry Slam. In that round, he read for 3 minutes and 11 seconds (you are only allowed to read for 3 minutes and 10 seconds). He received a one second time penalty. He placed second in the world that year. In 2008, he returned to The Individual World Poetry Slam and received a perfect score of 30 in the final round. He read for 3 minutes and 9 seconds. The following year he was the poet chosen to represent The United States of America at the European World Cup of Poetry Slam in Paris, France. He was lucky enough to win that competition as well. So we have it, the World Cup; (not the big one for soccer, which everyone else on the planet calls fútbol, but the small one for poetry) it rests on his wife's piano. He won it for you, so if you knock on his door and ask to hold it, he will let you. He snuck into the Sate Fair of Texas by climbing the fence behind the sideshow world of wonders tents from 1983 to 1987. He believes in God and prays for his children and wife often. He does not like to pray for himself. He is the son of a woman that he does not know well and the son of a man that he does not know at all. He was raised by his grandfather, who grew tomatoes, poems, and children in his small garden. He tends to vote Democratic. He believes the United States should have a uniform healthcare system similar to the ones that exist in France or Cuba. He likes movies where the protagonist finds hope in a hopeless situation. He has a photograph of him and Alicia Keys hugging each other. He will show it to you if you ask. He reads more than he writes and thinks that Suzanne Collins is a genius and will be taught in literature books hundreds of years from now. He co-wrote the book, *of fire and rain*, with natasha carrizosa. He thinks it is the best work he has ever created. He once saw a giant monarch butterfly dance with his daughter on the banks of the Trinity River. He counts this day as his best. In seventh grade, while

Toby and Jerome beat-boxed and rapped in the cafeteria during lunch, he attempted to make a name for himself as a break dancer, and challenged Ramón, a chubby, awkward kid from the barrio to a break dance battle. He would find out this day that Ramón was the lovechild of Ginger Rogers and Rerun from What's Happening. He lost this first battle, but not the war. In 1989 he met a Puerto Rican girl named Aída. That same year, he wrote her a short poem that reads, "Remember when I told you/that you are the kind of girl/that I could easily fall in love with/I did/I am." She still has the poem. He still has her.

Joaquín, the poet and teacher

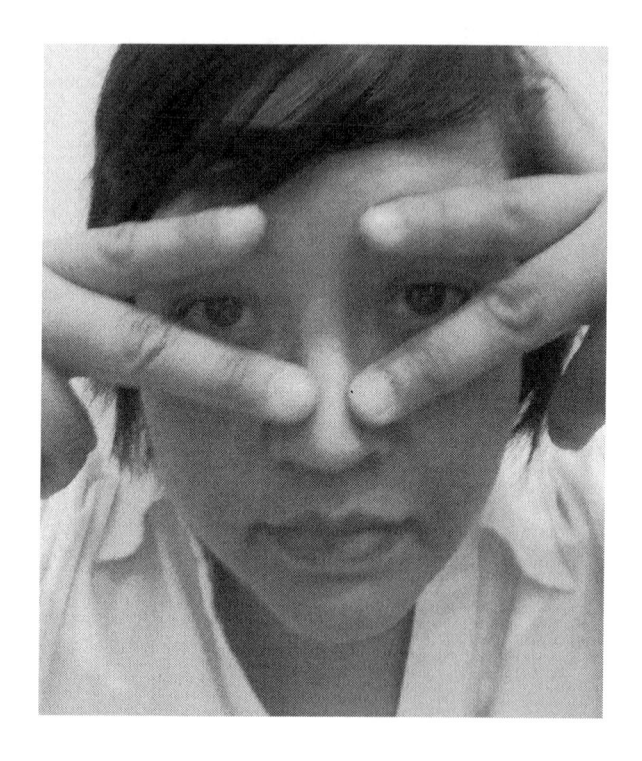

Aída, the designer and wife

Aiyana, the student and daughter

Dakota, the student and the other daughter

Nacho, the momma's boy, escape artist, and all around hellraiser

Acknowledgments

I must give thanks to all of the poets/friends/familia who act as human sounding boards offering me a platform and allowing me to recite poems to them while never tiring of giving me the feedback (*feedback, not criticism, you're right Chancelier there is a difference*) that I so desperately need. To Jonathan GNO White, my friend, my mentor, my coach, and the prototype by which all others should be measured, I say thank you for all that you have done/do/will do for me. To mi 'mana, natty, Natasha Carrizosa, who has taught me more than any other person I know about the craft and art of writing poetry, mil garcias 'mana. Thank you for always having my back, whether it's on the mean streets of Madrid or Paris or Funky Town. You have made me a better poet, but having you as my family has made me a better man. I have to offer gratitude to Roderick Rock Baby Goudy, who more than any other has taught me how to own a stage. Rock, if I were ever given a chance to pick my own poetry slam dream team, you would always be my first round daft choice. You've taught me more than you know. To Chancelier Xero Skidmore, I say you are one half mad and one half genius. All these years you and I have read poems to each other over the phone late at night, and I hope my insights were of some help to you. Yours certainly were to me.

To mi familia, mi Abuelo, mi madre, my tíos y tías, all of mi primos, y los mocosos that I used to run the streets of the barrio with, and even to you, father, I must let you all know that each and everyone of you shaped me into the poet and writer that I am today. I remember you all so vividly. It might be the way my youngest daughter laughs, or the way my oldest cries. It might be a song I've listened to or a poem I've read, but the memory of you lingers. And I have to let you know now, before it's too late, that to those of you that turned your back on me or didn't turn your back on me, if these poems say just one thing to you, let it be this, *I love you.*

To my daughters, Aiyana and Dakota, you make me smile more than anything on the planet. Know that you are both such a large part of this collection. Both of you on separate occasions have looked at the photo of my grandfather in my office and remarked how much you wished you could have met him. Both of you went on to say that you hope, if he is watching over you, that you have made him proud. There is no greater truth I can write than this, *you have*.

And finally to my beautiful Puerto Rican wife, Aída, know that you are my muse, none of these poems that I write came to me until I met you. It's fitting that I live with an artist, a gifted designer, because I find myself inspired by you, by your passion and creativity. The life that I have with you and our two daughters is a world away from that time when I was nothing more than a lost barrio boy who ran the streets desperate for something, someone to call his own. I finally know what it is to have a family tree. This is what you have given me. This is what you are to me, the roots from which our daughters grow and the limbs from which our future extends. You are the beginning and the end of everything for me, *remember when I said you are the kind of girl I could easily fall in love with, I did, I am.* Always.

Homework

     The teacher in me thought of the following pages as an opportunity to do just that…teach. So on the following pages will be a bit of homework for you the reader, or I guess at this point I should say the writer. My hope is that these poems have inspired you to put page to pen, and I wanted to provide you with room for that here in this book.

     In the age of the smart phone that we live in it is becoming a lost art form to actually put pen to page. But you should know there is something that the pen and the page have in their favor over the laptop or the smart phone. There is no delete button on the page. Yes you can strike through with one straight line at your leisure but the thing is that one line allows you the opportunity to go back and read what your first instinct was. It's a funny thing about first instincts, they're almost always right. Once you delete something off of a computer screen, there is a good chance that thought is gone forever.

     So since I have a lifetime teaching certification from the great state of Texas, that means I can give homework any time I like. So on the pages that follow I challenge you to write a line, a series of lines, an image, a thought, an idea, or even an actual poem. And since staring at a blank page can be as intimidating as standing on the edge of a cliff with the deep waters raging below beckoning you to take that leap of faith, I will include on each of the following pages a short writing prompt that I hope will act as jumping off point that allows you to dive into the process of writing the poem that may or may not change the world. So the rest of the book is yours. Your homework is to finish it. You have as many years as you have left to finish it, but why wait for tomorrow?

     The world is ready for change,
     let that change begin
     with the stroke of a pen.
     Write.
     The life you change
     may be your own.

                        —Joaquín Zihuatanejo

Haiku/Lowku

Write four haiku about four members of your family or four close friends. Remember haiku consist of 17 syllables, and the traditional form is five syllables on line one, seven on line two, and five on the third and final line. But don't get too caught up on form. Write just one in the traditional form and then break away from the traditional form and focus only on the 17 syllables using as many or as few lines as you like. To honor the ancient haiku masters who came before you, who often included in their haiku an element of nature, see if you can associate each family member or friend with some aspect of nature. But be passionate, raw, and gritty when you write. Don't be afraid to press the pen down hard, you just might leave an impression on someone you were not intending to impress.

Worth a Thousand Words

They say a picture is worth a thousand words. I think that the astonishing cover art to this book created by artist, Doug Seaman, is worth at least twice that, but remember you're writing a poem, so if you can say it 100 words instead of 500, say it in 100. Look at the cover art, which is titled, Tree of Life, for a minute, and then imagine you are the young one planted beneath. Now think of your family tree above you, around you, engulfing you on all sides. How does your family tree make you feel? Does it feel cumbersome? Heavy? Does it feel hopeful the way nourishment should truly feel? Write a companion poem for the cover art to this book from your perspective. See if you can tell your story and the story of your family tree as well. I have included the contact information for artist, Doug Seaman at the beginning of this collection. Feel free find him on Facebook or to send him a copy of your poem through email. I'm sure he would enjoy reading what his image inspired.

The Gift

Write a poem about a gift a family member has given to you. It might be an actual gift like a baseball glove or a flute, but it might be one of those intangible gifts that you can't see or touch like love, hope, or faith. You might find in the coming years that it is those gifts that make all the difference. See if in the poem you can tell the story of the gift, how it was given, what it meant/means to you, how you can perhaps give it away someday.

80s Mix Tape Meets Shakespeare

Okay for this collection I developed a very simplistic and Americanized version of the sonnet, focusing not on the rhyme and meter of the sonnet, but just on the transitions. A sonnet has three distinct parts, the first eight lines called the octet, the next six lines called the sestet, and the last two lines called the couplet. Tell your life story in 14 songs. Make each line the title of the song. Make song one your birth and song 14 your death. Focus on your youth and maturation in the octet and your adulthood and the love of your life in the first part of the sestet. Concentrate on your old age and death in the couplet. Don't do this haphazardly. Ache over it, the way a teenager in the 80s would ache over the process of making that special someone in his life the perfect mix tape. Consider challenging someone you love to do the same. You could even have a mix tape biographical sonnet party where you and your guests listen to selections from your life. So Record/Play/Pause/Stop/Go.

"Half and Half but Whole"

The astonishing American poet, Natasha Carrizosa has a poem entitled, "mejiafricana" in which she tells the story of both halves of herself. One half coming from her African American mother, the other half from her father who was born in Mexico. She tells the story of her people, su gente, realizing at the poem's conclusion that she is "half and half but whole." In part of the space below draw a line and on one side of the line list traits and characteristics of your father and his family, his people, on the other side of the line do the same for your mother. After you've done this write a poem that tells the story of both halves of you. If there is a conflict there, find a way by the poem's end that resolution might be reached.

Family Photo

Find an old family photo album, not an album of photos on Twitter or Facebook, but an actual photo album that belongs to your father, or your grandmother, or any family member for that matter and flip through the pages until you find a photo that forces you to stop turning pages because that photo, which has so much to say, is speaking to you. Write a poem about that photo; in the poem describe what's in the frame and what's just outside of it. See if you can tell the story of this place or these people in your poem. You may have to do some research if it contains people or places you are not familiar with.

Conflict Resolution

If there is one person in your family that you have a conflict with, try to imagine that conflict from their point of view. Now write a poem from their perspective about the riff between the two of you. You might even have that person speak directly to you in the poem. Think of their mannerisms and speech patterns; try to be as honest and faithful as you can, even if it hurts.

The Extended Metaphor

Write a conceit, or an extended metaphor, about a family member. I do this in the title poem of this collection, "Family Tree." For this exercise start with a metaphor near the top of the poem and stretch it down the length of the poem. Do not come back to that comparison on every line or you will beat the reader up with simile and metaphor, but rather come back to the comparison every third or fourth line. At all costs avoid clichés. Make your metaphors and similes odd, twisted, and beautiful…like you. A good poet to read to inspire you is Sharon Olds, who is an American master of metaphor and simile.

Imagine the Imagery

Imagery is defined as sensory details. These are instances that when you think of them you can almost touch them, smell them, taste them, or see them because they are so alive with memory. List the names of your family members and out to the side of each name write down the smell, sight, touch, and taste that you most associate with each family member. These might be pleasant or unpleasant images. Remember the poems that hurt to write are almost always the best and the most healing. After completing the list look at it and choose the one that is most alive with memories and write a poem that captures that memory or the connection that exists between the two of you. Remember to bring the poem to life with sensory details.

Looking Forward by Looking Back

Research the life of a family who died before you got a chance to know them. For this research you may use periodicals, newspapers, and online resources, but I hope you won't. I hope you'll actually strap on your Chucks and get out in the world and interview family members face to face who can tell you stories about the person in question. (If you live a great distance from most family members you can always Skype them or even simply call them.) Allow them to laugh and cry with you as you take notes on that person's life and then after a few interviews see if you can write a poem that paints a vivid portrait of this person's life.

They Are Because They Did

Remember the quote, "I think; therefore, I am." We often associate a person's identity, a person's story with what they do or did. Write a poem about a family member that tells their story by telling us what they did. Use diction, or words, very specific to their trade or profession. If they were a welder, research terminology specific to that line of work, and incorporate some of those interesting words into the poem. Here's a short poem to conclude this collection that I hope serves as inspiration to you, while honoring the family member I'm addressing in the poem.

Elegy for a Dancer

for Ann who lost her brother and for Nancy who lost the other half of herself

"Let us read and dance—
two amusements that will never do any harm to the world."

—Voltaire

How tragic to lose such a soul
A man who made poetry with the soles
Of his feet
That were another form of drum beat
There was music in his eyes
So it's no wonder that his limbs
Found the rhythm of the world around him
And it's true what they say about a time for everything
A time to weep and a time to laugh
A time to mourn and a time to dance
And when the evening breeze falls on your face
Let the dancing wind be his embrace
So think of him this way
With the joy of the world
In the twist of his hips
It will be the song of his dance
That you feel on your lips

—Joaquín Zihuatanejo